BEST AUSTRALIAN POLITICAL CARTOONS 2016

Russ Radcliffe created the annual *Best Australian Political Cartoons* series in 2003. His other books include *Man of Steel: a cartoon history of the Howard Years* in 2007; *Dirt Files: a decade of Australian Political Cartoons* in 2013; and *My Brilliant Career: Malcolm Turnbull, a political life in cartoons* in 2016.

Russ has edited collections from some of Australia's finest political cartoonists, including Matt Golding, Judy Horacek, Bill Leak, Alan Moir, and Bruce Petty, and curated exhibitions including *Moments of Truth*, *Dirt Files*, and *Suppositories of Wisdom*.

In 2013, Russ was awarded the Australian Cartoonists Association's Jim Russell Award for his contribution to Australian cartooning — a bit embarrassing, as he can't draw to save his life.

For political cartoonists everywhere: an endangered species

BEST AUSTRALIAN POLITICAL CARTOONS

2016

edited by

Russ Radcliffe

SCRIBE
Melbourne • London

Scribe Publications
18–20 Edward St, Brunswick, Victoria 3056, Australia
2 John St, Clerkenwell, London, WC1N 2ES, United Kingdom

Published by Scribe 2016

Printed and bound in Australia by OPUS Group

Scribe Publications is committed to the sustainable use of natural resources and the use of paper products made responsibly from those resources.

ISBN 9781925321760 (pbk.)

A CiP record for this title is available from the National Library of Australia.

scribepublications.com.au
scribepublications.co.uk

Front cover image: Jon Kudelka, *www.kudelka.com.au*
Back cover image: Andrew Dyson, *The Age*

Commissioned
and produced by

High Horse
books

www.highhorse.com.au
russ@highhorse.com.au

Cartoonists

David Rowe, *Australian Financial Review*

Introduction

When Malcolm Turnbull finally seized the prime ministership from Tony Abbott, the nation, as one commentator suggested, breathed a sigh of relief. He seemed to promise a way out of the dead end of uncompromising vendetta politics and the brutal sloganeering and social conservatism that had defined Abbott's tenure as opposition leader and as PM. If his defenestration upset the conservative elements of the Liberal Party, it carried none of the stigma of Kevin Rudd's removal among an electorate desperate for an intelligent, adult politics.

Turnbull seemed to hold the magic key (p. 12) that would unlock the aspirations and desires of so many small 'l' liberal and progressive interests frozen out from Abbott conservatism: on climate change, gay marriage, asylum seekers, the republic, etc.

The expectations were enormous. And unrealistic. Malcolm as PM was not the leather-jacketed wit dog-whistling to the centre-left on *Q&A*. Nor was he the high-handed Malcolm of 2009 steamrolling a recalcitrant party; he had learned the hazards of that approach – perhaps too well. Holding his heavily factionalised party together meant appeasing, or at least not antagonising, the Abbott loyalists and Barnaby's Nationals on his back.

In a tedious recurrence of recent history, we witnessed a nervous new PM unable to appeal to the record of the government he inherited, and also – with a good proportion of its former and current members gunning for him – unable to reject it. The vacuous mantra stolen from American TV, 'continuity with change', just highlighted the dilemma and invited ridicule.

So it was year zero – again. Everything, famously, was on the table (p. 64).

Well, not quite everything. Not that stuff beloved of ABC watchers and latte elites. Only the serious economic reforms required to prepare us all for transition to a post-minerals 'Australia of the future'.

The danger of the strategy soon became apparent. When everything is on the table, everyone is potentially a loser and susceptible to being spooked. Debates about increasing the GST and negative gearing came and went, and a proposal to extend income-taxing powers to the states – a fundamental change in the relationship between the states and federal governments – floated and sank within a few days, in a fashion that suggested there was no controlling intelligence behind the proposals. The impression was of government by thought balloon, adrift and indecisive, with a treasurer and PM unable to communicate.

Reg Lynch, *The Sun-Herald*

Labor, initially in shock from losing their favoured opponent, energetically bounced back. The comparison with the Labor Party's apparent confidence and ambitious agenda was apparent.

Patience, people said. Malcolm needed to secure a mandate in his own right to quieten the factional wolves before embarking on his a long-term project to return the Liberal Party to its more classical small 'l' liberal roots.

Yeah, but no. In reality, the thrill was gone; the honeymoon well and truly over (p. 91).

By the time the double dissolution election was called (p. 106), all the Coalition had left on its reform table were changes to superannuation – significant enough to panic its own base – and a promise to cut corporate taxes in the long term. How this would magically stimulate economic agility and creativity was never quite explained.

The longest campaign in Australian electoral history could also lay claim to being the most vacuous. Campaign slogans are usually more desire than blueprint, but with the endless repetition of 'jobs and growth' it seemed the Coalition's strategy was to have us sleepwalk into the booths. Labor's late 'Mediscare' campaign certainly woke them up, and almost stole the election. The Coalition's outrage at such a tactic was laughably hypocritical, with the grandmaster of the art of the political dogfight still sitting on their backbench.

Turnbull's audacious double-dissolution strategy failed on all counts (p. 139). A win is a win, but it didn't feel like it to the Coalition. It neither delivered a more manageable Senate, nor maintained the government's position, nor shored up Turnbull's moral authority in the party.

•

But it wasn't all about Malcolm. Dissatisfaction with the economics of globalisation and the deeply uneven spread of its benefits – apparent in Britain's decision to leave the EU (p. 150) and in the anti-TPP policies of Donald Trump and Hillary Clinton – was also reflected in the success of populist protectionist attitudes of the Nick Xenophon Team and One Nation.

'Mr Harbourside Mansion's' claims that there 'has never been a more exciting time to be an Australian' and corporate-speak admonishments to make 'disruption' our friend might have cut it in an inner-urban start-up, but it was always going to fall flat with a newly unemployed steelworker. The losers from the imagined panacea of more and more free trade in goods and capital are clearly a new force to be reckoned with in modern politics.

Paul Zanetti, *www.zanetti.net.au*

The new residents of the 45th Parliament look like being an obstreperous bunch, and politics looks likely to be more dissonant than ever. There are loud appeals from within and without the government on a range of issues that threaten to divert and fragment its attention: the repeal of section 18C of the Racial Discrimination Act; the plebiscite on gay marriage; a royal commission into juvenile detention and a demand for one into the banks; the

Alan Moir, *The Sydney Morning Herald*

continuing disgrace of offshore detention; as well as bizarre calls for inquiries into Islam and claims about a NASA-led conspiracy on climate science.

The possibility of a consensus, or at least acquiescence, on a range of critical economic reforms amid all these distractions will require a level of political agility and deliberative skill that we haven't seen from the Coalition, notwithstanding Turnbull's claim to lead an adult, consultative government.

The emboldened conservative factions of the Liberal Party still smart from the removal of their champion, distrust the PM's ideas, and resent his leadership. For Malcolm Turnbull, the road ahead is likely to be arduous. Thoughtfully, he has set the numerical bar for the assessment of his prime-ministerial performance. Justifying his move on Tony Abbott, he said, 'We have lost 30 Newspolls in a row. It is clear that the people have made up their mind about Mr Abbott's leadership.'

It is clear that Turnbull's enemies have already started counting.

•

Bill Leak has always plied his trade on provocation's bleeding edge. As a result, he is no stranger to the righteously indignant, from relatively harmless excrement-smeared letters during the Howard years to Islamist-inspired death threats in more recent times. These days, it is more likely the left who are affronted, and the medium of attack has switched, less consequentially, to Twitter.

Leak's depiction of a drunken Aboriginal father who doesn't recognise his own wayward son was published in the immediate wake of ABC TV's *Four Corners* revelations about the Don Dale youth detention centre. No cartoon in recent memory has been more contentious (p. 174).

The image of the restrained and hooded boy rapidly acquired that rare literal and metaphoric power able to penetrate the fog of the modern mediascape, and the indifference it breeds, into the national conscience, much as photos of Iraqi prisoners at Abu Ghraib had a decade earlier.

If Warren Brown (p. 170) explicitly connects Don Dale to the brutalities of our racist past, Leak shifts the focus from the historical and structural to the present and the personal suggesting that the road to incarceration starts with dysfunctional Aboriginal families and a failure of 'personal responsibility'.

As Peter Nicholson remarked, no cartoon can tell the whole truth. Indeed, but bearer of a partial truth or not, and irrelevant of intent, images such as this

John Farmer, *Mercury*

don't stand innocently outside of history. They automatically plug into and draw their metaphoric power from an inglorious lineage of Indigenous representations and explicitly racialist explanations.

Did Leak's gate-crashing of an all-too-familiar festival of outrage achieve what political cartoons are supposed to do – that is, cut through the predictable confections of public discourse? Leak certainly believes so and, further, that this crucial incendiary vitality has been lost in the inoffensive and enfeebled platitudes required by 'political correctness'.

Worthy or not, Leak's cartoon came at a time when demands for the repeal of section 18C of the Racial Discrimination Act were again being revived, and it became a topic for satire in its own right (p. 175 & p. 178). David Pope ties it into the Olympics and the electoral success of One Nation, with Leak as the flag carrier for an anachronistic Australian team of right-wing fringe dwellers.

Who says cartoons are harmless fun?

•

This year there have been many losses in the ranks of Australian cartoonists as news and media organisations become ever more attenuated. Political cartooning as we have known it – as a professionally validated means of social and political commentary – is seriously threatened. Of course, it's not just tough for cartoonists; we are witnessing the passing of a whole culture of print journalism as great writers, researchers, editors, illustrators, designers, etc. move on.

But, as David Pope said, this year particularly it has felt like 'notice was being served on the craft'. It does indeed feel like this brilliant form of social and political commentary is being undermined by the very people who ought to at least appreciate, if not love, it.

It is invidious to select individual cartoonists in the midst of this carnage, but I must pay special tribute to three who have left longstanding positions on major newspapers this year. Bruce Petty, John Spooner, and Peter Nicholson are among the finest practitioners of this crazy art Australia has produced. Their artistic styles are distinctive and their ideological perspectives are often at odds, but they share a belief in the seriousness and significance of their craft. The idea that their editorial cartoons and caricatures are just a bit of a giggle and a piss-take would be entirely anathema to them.

Their work on the Iraq war demonstrated to me the possibilities of this great art of satirical commentary, and renewed my interest in political cartooning – inspiring me to start this annual *Best Australian Political Cartoons* collection in 2003. They have been at the heart of these books ever since.

I am sure such agile, innovative, and creative characters will find new avenues for their brilliance.

Russ Radcliffe

John Spooner, *The Age*

David Pope, *The Canberra Times*

'This will be a thoroughly Liberal Government. It will be a thoroughly Liberal Government committed to freedom, the individual, and the market. It will be focused on ensuring that in the years ahead, as the world becomes more and more competitive, and greater opportunities arise, we are able to take advantage of that. The Australia of the future has to be a nation that is agile, that is innovative, that is creative.

'We cannot be defensive, we cannot future proof ourselves. We have to recognise that the disruption that we see driven by technology, the volatility and change is our friend, is our friend if we are agile and smart enough to take advantage of it. There has never been a more exciting time to be alive than today, and there has never been a more exciting time to be an Australian.'

— Malcolm Turnbull, PM

First Dog on the Moon,
The Guardian

Matt Golding, *The Sunday Age*

'A strong result in Canning – which is what we were going to get – would have put paid to this notion that somehow I was unelectable because of the polls.'
– Tony Abbott, MP

'This campaign was always about the people of Canning and their concerns. It is quite clear that the people of Canning don't care about Canberra politicking or tricky games and it is worth noting that London and Moscow are actually closer together than Perth and Canberra themselves.'
– Andrew Hastie, MP for Canning

'The truth is we are never going to know what the result would have been if we had not changed leaders on Monday night … This is a great victory for the Liberal Party under the leadership of Malcolm Turnbull.'
– Mathias Cormann, finance minister

Geoff Pryor, *The Saturday Paper*

'There will be no wrecking, no undermining, and no sniping. I've never leaked or backgrounded against anyone, and I certainly won't start now …

'We have more polls and more commentary than ever before. Mostly sour, bitter, character assassination. Poll-driven panic has produced a revolving-door prime ministership, which can't be good for our country. And a febrile media culture has developed that rewards treachery.'

— Tony Abbott, MP

'It was very, very gut-wrenching. It was devastating. It's a devastating business, a terribly cruel business, politics. Because all of your mistakes and blunders are out there in the public arena. You've got nowhere to hide. There is not an ounce of privacy.'

— Malcolm Turnbull, deposed opposition leader, 2013

Pat Campbell, *The Canberra Times*

John Farmer, *Mercury*

Cathy Wilcox, *The Sun-Herald*

Matt Golding, *The Sunday Age*

David Pope, *The Canberra Times*

'We need a style of leadership that … respects the people's intelligence, that explains these complex issues and then sets out the course of action we believe we should take and makes a case for it. We need advocacy, not slogans. We need to respect the intelligence of the Australian people.'

— Malcolm Turnbull, PM

'There's no doubt the country is breathing a sigh of relief.'

— Jason Clare, MP

'I don't bear grudges. I'm not a hater. Some politicians are highly motivated by hatred and animosity, but it rots away at them. I'll sound like some counter-cultural hippy, but I know a lot of people in politics who have destroyed themselves and become miserable and bitter because they've allowed themselves to be consumed by hatred and resentment.'

— Malcolm Turnbull, PM

Matt Golding, *The Sunday Age*

Matt Golding, *The Sunday Age*

Dean Alston, *The West Australian*

'The whole driving purpose of my political life is a rather corny one. And that is: a commitment to public service, a belief that what I'm doing is important and that I'm making a contribution to ensuring Australia enhances its reputation, preserves its prosperity, and remains a great country to live in now, and into the future.'

— Malcolm Turnbull, PM

'Turnbull might be the left's ideal Liberal leader, but his own party is more likely to junk him than its principles, even if it means losing office.'

— Peta Credlin, commentator

'I think it's really important that Malcolm Turnbull doesn't change his views that he had when he was the sort of Liberal gadfly giving Tony Abbott a hard time, and I hope that he sticks true to his views.'

— Bill Shorten, opposition leader

Ron Tandberg, *The Age*

Fiona Katauskas, *Eureka Street*

David Rowe, *Australian Financial Review*

'We should never as members of the Liberal Party of Australia lose sight of the fact that we are the trustees of two great political traditions ... the classical liberal tradition ... [and] the conservative tradition in our community. And if you look at the history of the Liberal Party, it is at its best when it balances and blends those two traditions.'

— John Howard

'Malcolm Turnbull has grown through his parliamentary career. I think his defeat for the leadership in 2010 was a traumatic event for him. I think it's made him think about himself and the country, and I think he'll be a better leader for that having happened. The real question is: can he now take the now very right-wing Liberal Party anywhere back near the centre? That'll be the real test. Or whether he's stuck with the Looney Tunes show on the right.'

— Paul Keating

Alan Moir, *The Sydney Morning Herald*

Alan Moir, *The Sydney Morning Herald*

Peter Broelman, *broelman.com.au*

'The Nationals have always had respect for the PM. We don't want to be divisive figures fighting our own government, but we will push for the best outcomes for regional people.'
— Barnaby Joyce, deputy PM

'Barnaby and I are here on our road trip … It's not Thelma and Louise, it's Barnaby and Malcolm, but we're on the road trip and we're having a great time.'
— Malcolm Turnbull, PM

'We are a business partnership and not a marriage. At certain times, the business partners have different views on things, but I'm not going to go searching for them.'
— Barnaby Joyce, deputy PM

'They're yin and yang in politics.'
— Christopher Pyne, defence industry minister

Christopher Downes, *Mercury*

Dean Alston, *The West Australian*

Ron Tandberg, *The Age*

'We are not run by factions [laughter]. Well, you may dispute that, but I have to tell you, from experience, we are not run by factions, nor are we run by big business, or by deals in back rooms. We rely on the ideas and the energy and enterprise of our membership …

'We endeavour to take those values, turn them into policy, to win government and hold government and in doing so, we do that with no object in mind other than the advancement of Australia.

'Tony Abbott has held firm to those Liberal values throughout his career and public life. He held true to them as an opposition leader, he held true to them as prime minister …

'He took us out of the wilderness of opposition and took us back into government and achieved great things, great reforms, great commitments … all of us owe him an enormous debt.'

— Malcolm Turnbull, PM

Pat Campbell, *The Canberra Times*

Christopher Downes, *Mercury*

Pat Campbell, *The Canberra Times*

'One of the great challenges for any leader is to ensure that there is renewal. That we are able to bring up new talent, new faces, into leadership positions over time, and that often means – that invariably means, in fact – that very capable people have to move on, stand aside so that owners can come through.'

– Malcolm Turnbull, PM

'It is understandable that with the removal of Tony Abbott, Kevin Andrews, and myself from the ministry that our core constituency feels disenfranchised and concerned that their views will no longer be heard ... I will continue to be a strong advocate for the grassroots of our cause and what we believe in, albeit from the backbench.'

– Senator Eric Abetz

Glen Le Lievre, *The Sun-Herald*

'These aberrations cannot be regarded as isolated. They are not the work of a few rogue unions, or a few rogue officials ... It would be utterly naïve to think that what has been uncovered is anything other than the small tip of an enormous iceberg. It is clear that in many parts of the world constituted by Australian trade-union officials, there is room for louts, thugs, bullies, thieves, perjurers, those who threaten violence, errant fiduciaries, and organisers of boycotts.'

— Justice Dyson Heydon, Trade Union Royal Commission (TURC)

'This is the last feather with which some of the crossbench are seeking to fly to vote against the ABCC legislation, and my view was that last feather should be plucked out, then they would have no feathers to fly with at all and they would be duty-bound to support the ABCC legislation.'

— Senator Eric Abetz

Bill Leak, *The Australian*

Bill Leak, *The Australian*

Mark Knight, *Herald Sun*

'This poll is not so much a sugar hit as a liver transplant for the Coalition. And unfortunately for Bill Shorten, he happens to be the donor.'

— Nick Xenophon, MP

'I think it's a good thing for this country that Tony Abbott is no longer prime minister of Australia. Of course, I would have liked to have been the one to have replaced Tony Abbott, because whoever did replace Tony Abbott was going to get a boost in the polls as they say.'

— Bill Shorten, opposition leader

'The Labor Party runs the real risk that .... if Malcolm Turnbull can shift those pre-Copernican obscurantists in his party at all, and they give him a bit of room to move towards the centre, that will present great strategic difficulties for the Labor Party.'

— Paul Keating

Fiona Katauskas, *Eureka Street*

Matt Golding, *The Sunday Age*

Reg Lynch, *The Sun-Herald*

Cathy Wilcox, *The Sun-Herald*

Matt Golding, *The Sunday Age*

'I'm going to see if I can cancel Malcolm's visa so he stays over there for a little while.'
— Barnaby Joyce, acting PM

'The bloke's a fool. Some of the things that come out of his mouth are embarrassing. There's no policy depth to him. I think he's a goose.'
— Tony Windsor

'No great country has the monarch of another country as their head of state. No great country has the flag of another country in the corner of their flag.'
— Paul Keating

'I've led a "yes" case for a republic into a heroic defeat once. I've got no desire to do so again.'
— Malcolm Turnbull, PM

Geoff Pryor, *The Saturday Paper*

'Cape Grim is the world's sentinel for measuring the atmosphere's carbon-dioxide levels. When Cape Grim records 400 ppm, it will mean that the entire planet's atmosphere will have passed a critical marker.'
— Senator Peter Whish-Wilson

'It would be great if we could fund everybody. But given the finite envelope — both appropriation, government funding, and external revenue — we've got to shift the emphasis from the measurement and modelling to the mitigation and adaptation.'
— Dr Larry Marshall, CEO of CSIRO

'It turns out you can't run a long-standing public institution like a Silicon Valley start-up.'
— Adam Bandt, MP

Cathy Wilcox, *The Sun-Herald*

Alan Moir, *The Sydney Morning Herald*

Judy Horacek, *The Age*

'I do think there has been a war on science to some extent, an attack on climate scientists. Ignoring what the CSIRO says and ignoring what leading scientists say and discounting it all is silly.'
— Malcolm Turnbull, MP, 2011

'People who don't believe in climate change have taken over the Liberal party ... What more evidence do you need to see the harmful effects of climate change than the damage being done to the Barrier Reef?'
— Bill Shorten, opposition leader

'Everyone thought it would be a breath of fresh air when Turnbull kicked out Abbott ... It seemed like a beacon of enlightenment was about to be rained down upon us. It's been shattering, I think, to see how things have deteriorated under the Turnbull government, and surprises myself and everybody.'
— Michael Borgas, CSIRO Staff Association

THE FINAL ACT WILL BE THE NERO FIDDLERS PERFORMING THE GLOBAL WARMING CONCERTO

Lindsay Foyle, *New Matilda*

Ron Tandberg, *The Age*

Bill Leak, *The Australian*

David Pope, *The Canberra Times*

'Our world today needs ministers to serve as role models of thought and action, which bring about progress and welfare and improve general societal well-being.'
— Greg Hunt, 'The Best Minister In The World'

'Paris will produce an outcome of about 2.7 degrees, but everybody is committed to the Paris process to review national targets.'
— Greg Hunt, environment minister

'Hallelujah. The world is saved ... The polar bears can sleep soundly tonight.'
— Craig Kelly, MP

'The Coalition's denialist dinosaurs continue to run the Turnbull government just as they did under Tony Abbott.'
— Adam Bandt, MP

Jon Kudelka, *www.kudelka.com.au*

'Recent experience in Australia had shown that negative commentary about the status of world heritage properties impacted on tourism.'
— environment-department statement

'It's very rare that I would see something like this … Perhaps in the old Soviet Union you would see this sort of thing happening, where governments would quash information because they didn't like it. But not in western democracies. I haven't seen it happen before.'
— Prof. Will Steffen

'It's hard to tell the difference between an alarmist claim about global effects and the basic premise of a disaster-movie plot. When we are in a flood, they tell us too much rain is a sign; more hurricanes is a sign; fewer hurricanes is a sign; the sky is blue it's a sign; gravity — it's a sign.'
— George Christensen, MP

Pat Campbell, *The Canberra Times*

Glen Le Lievre, *The Sun-Herald*

John Spooner, *The Age*

'If I was a guy, I wouldn't be bossy: I'd be strong. If I was a guy, I wouldn't be a micro manager: I'd be across my brief or across the detail. You know, if I wasn't strong, determined, controlling – and got them into government from opposition, I might add – then I would be weak and not up to it.'

– Peta Credlin, commentator

'Do you really think that if I sacked Credlin and Hockey, Malcolm Turnbull would have stopped wanting to be prime minister?'

– Tony Abbott, MP

'Tony Abbott and Peta Credlin were the architects of their own downfall. It is convenient, but it is not true to blame others or to use the gender card to try to explain why they were tipped out of office.'

– Niki Savva, *The Road to Ruin*

Mark Knight, *Herald Sun*

Glen Le Lievre, *The Sun-Herald*

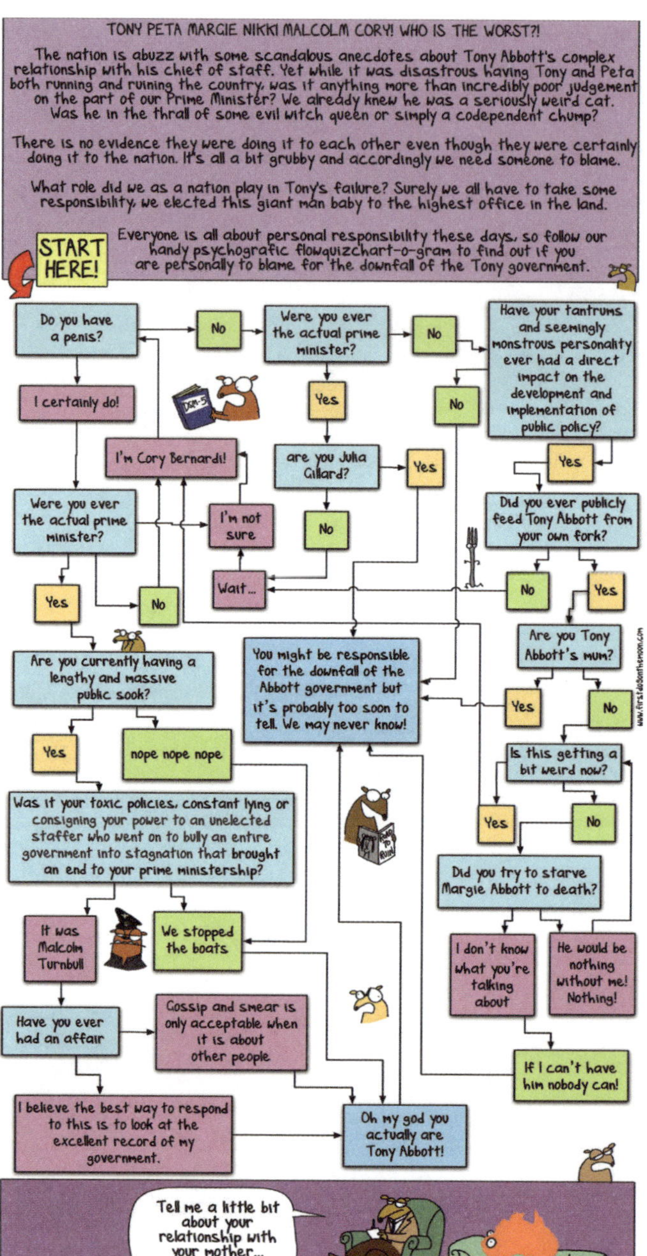

First Dog on the Moon,
The Guardian

David Rowe, *Australian Financial Review*

'It would be terrible if people were to abandon the Coalition because of this. It's always better to stay in and fight. I can appreciate that there are a lot of people out there who are dismayed by what's happened, but, as I said, it would be even worse if we were to end up with a sixth prime minister in six years. Even if they have to do it through gritted teeth, support the Coalition, support the prime minister, support the government.'
— Tony Abbott, MP

'The betrayal of you [Kevin Rudd] as leader of your party was one of the most shocking events I have ever witnessed ... The idea that the man who had won, in this presidential campaign, an election against John Howard was then going to be disposed of, discarded like another course on a lazy Susan in a Vietnamese restaurant — the cruelty of it was extraordinary!'
— Malcolm Turnbull, MP, 2013

Geoff Pryor, *The Saturday Paper*

'Tony, you brought to an end the chaos and dysfunction of the, Rudd-Gillard-Rudd years, and you remain a powerful and dedicated advocate too for our great cause ... Tony we salute you.'
— Malcolm Turnbull, PM

'The point I've made again and again, and let me repeat it here, is that the Abbott era is over and the Liberal Party rightly wants to look forward, not back. Now, I certainly want to be a constructive contributor to that process. I certainly do want to be a constructive contributor to that process, and I think there's a lot that I can do over the next three years to try to crystallise and clarify where centre-right politics in this country goes from here. But in terms of the top job, the Abbott era, as I've said before, is well and truly over.'
— Tony Abbott, MP

David Pope, *The Canberra Times*

David Pope, *The Canberra Times*

Bill Leak, *The Australian*

Andrew Dyson, *The Age*

Jon Kudelka, *www.kudelka.com.au*

'The enmities are so deep, the wrongs so shocking, that every option should be on the table ... This is a time for creative pragmatism and a recognition that difficult compromises will be required, particularly to avoid the sectarian aspect of this struggle spreading more widely across the region.'
— Malcolm Turnbull, PM

'We have to constantly lift our game in the way we engage with and tackle these extremists, particularly ISIL — but there are many others — as they operate in the cyber sphere. Archaic and barbaric though they may be, their use regrettably of the internet is very sophisticated.'
— President Barack Obama

'The cyber sphere demands reactions as rapid as the kinetic battlefield. We are working with our partners in South-East Asia to improve the effectiveness of our counter-narrative online, and I was pleased to see heightened cooperation here in Washington between the government and the private-sector telcos, software developers, and social-media platforms to that end.'
— Malcolm Turnbull, PM

John Spooner, *The Age*

Bill Leak, *The Australian*

'As Margaret Thatcher so clearly understood over the Falklands, those that won't use decisive force, where needed, end up being dictated to by those who will. Of course, no American or British or Australian parent should face bereavement in a fight far away. But what is the alternative? Leaving anywhere, even Syria, to the collective determination of Russia, Iran, and Daesh should be too horrible to contemplate.'

— Tony Abbott, MP

'The United States military deserves a commander-in-chief who loves our country passionately, and will never apologise for this country ... just last week, we're watching our sailors suffer and be humiliated on a world stage at the hands of Iranian captors in violation of international law, because a weak-kneed, capitulator-in-chief has decided that America will lead from behind ... sends a message to the rest of the world that they capture and we kowtow, and we apologise, and then, we bend over and say, "Thank you, enemy."'

— Sarah Palin

First Dog on the Moon,
The Guardian

Bruce Petty, *The Age*

'We've got to work closely with live-and-let-live Muslims because there needs to be, as president Al-Sisi of Egypt has said, a religious revolution inside Islam. All of those things that Islam has never had — a Reformation, an Enlightenment, a well-developed concept of the separation of church and state — that needs to happen.But we can't do it; Muslims have got to do this for themselves ...

'All cultures are not equal and, frankly, a culture that believes in decency and tolerance is much to be preferred to one which thinks that you can kill in the name of God, and we've got to be prepared to say that.'

— Tony Abbott, MP

'Tony Abbott just called for both a Reformation and a revolution "within Islam". This is, of course, perhaps the most well-worn and ill-informed cliche of Western discourse on Islam — the kind of thing people like to say when they want to sound serious but know almost exactly nothing about Islam, Muslim societies, or, indeed, the Reformation.'

— Waleed Aly, commentator

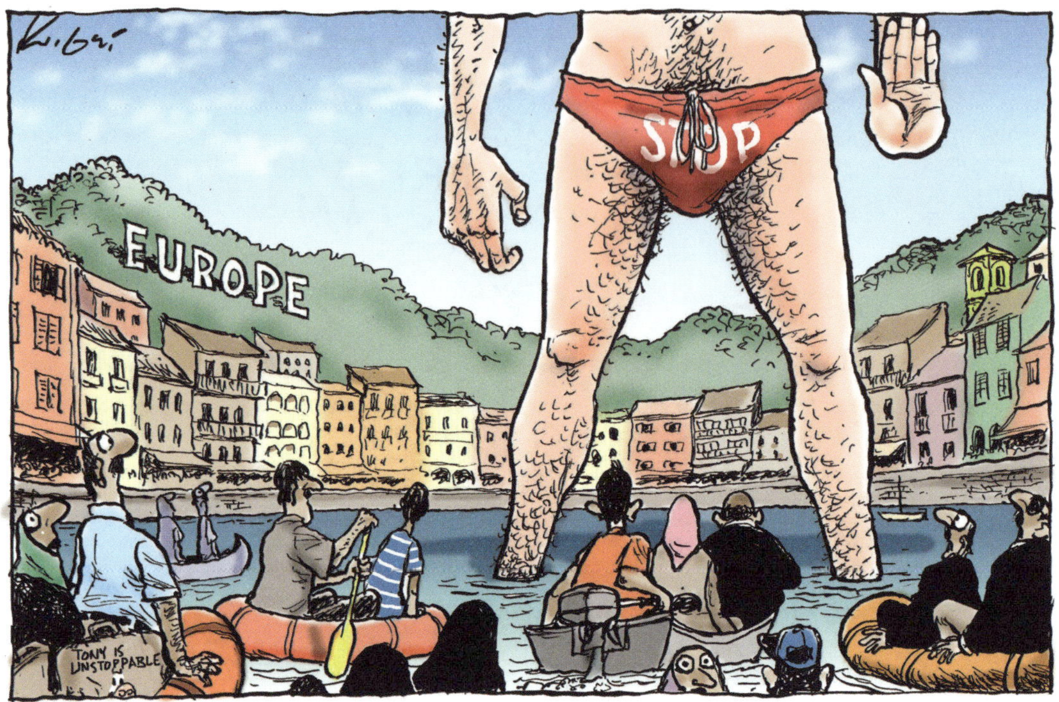

Mark Knight, *Herald Sun*

'I'm happy that Germany has become a country that many people abroad associate with hope. That is something very valuable, especially in view of our history.'
— Chancellor Angela Merkel

'The German people are going to riot. The German people are going to end up overthrowing that woman.'
— Donald Trump, US presidential candidate

'Implicitly or explicitly, the imperative to "love your neighbour as you love yourself" is at the heart of every Western polity ... but right now this wholesome instinct is leading much of Europe into catastrophic error ... It will require some force; it will require massive logistics and expense; it will gnaw at our consciences — yet it is the only way to prevent a tide of humanity surging through Europe and quite possibly changing it forever. We are rediscovering the hard way that justice tempered by mercy is an exacting ideal as too much mercy for some necessarily undermines justice for all.'
— Tony Abbott, MP

Alan Moir, *The Sydney Morning Herald*

Alan Moir, *The Sydney Morning Herald*

Warren Brown, *The Daily Telegraph*

'My dear compatriots – as I speak, terrorist attacks of unprecedented proportions are underway in the Paris area. There are dozens killed; there are many injured. It is a horror.'
– President François Hollande

'Whoever stands in the ranks of Kufr [unbelievers] will be a target for our swords and will fall in humiliation.'
– ISIS video

'To all those who have seen these awful things, I want to say we are going to lead a war which will be pitiless. Because when terrorists are capable of committing such atrocities, they must be certain that they are facing a determined France, a united France, a France that is together and does not let itself be moved, even if today we express infinite sorrow.'
– President François Hollande

John Spooner, *The Age*

Ron Tandberg, *The Age*

John Spooner, *The Age*

'We have come to you with slaughter, and indeed our knives come closer to your throats day after day ... I send a message now to those remaining in France who claim to be Muslims. By Allah, I ask myself what you are doing there. We are being killed every day and you are there sitting idly, living among them, sleeping among them, eating with them, with these disbelievers, while it is within your ability to display some honor and spit in their faces – if you can't find a weapon – or smash their heads with a rock, or run them over with your car and terrorise them.'

– Samy Amimour, Paris attacks

'The Nazis did terrible evil but they had a sufficient sense of shame to try to hide it. These people boast about their evil – this is the extraordinary thing. They act in the way that medieval barbarians acted, only they broadcast it to the world with an effrontery which is hard to credit.'

– Tony Abbott, MP

Pat Campbell, *The Canberra Times*

Dean Alston, *The West Australian*

Jon Kudelka, *www.kudelka.com.au*

'We consider the border not to be a purely physical barrier separating nation states, but a complex continuum stretching offshore and onshore, including the overseas, maritime, physical border and domestic dimensions of the border.'

— *Who We Are*, Australian Border Force

'This is how tired we are — this action will prove how exhausted we are. I cannot take it anymore.'

— Omid Masoumali, Iranian refugee who died from self-inflicted burns

'I refuse to accept that this is the best we can do. There are not just the two options of dangerous boat journeys or people burning themselves to death.'

— Senator Sarah Hanson-Young

Cathy Wilcox, *The Sun-Herald*

Cathy Wilcox, *The Sun-Herald*

David Rowe, *Australian Financial Review*

'Refugee advocates must stop giving refugees and asylum seekers on Nauru false hope and stirring up these protests. They are making the situation worse and must take responsibility for their actions and words.'
— Peter Dutton, immigration minister

'The Turnbull government's policy, focused only on deterrence with no feasible pathway to permanent migration in a resettlement country, is leaving people desperate and without hope.'
— Richard Marles, Labor's immigration spokesman

'Far from living in the hell hole advocates would have you believe — refugees on Nauru are free from a fear of persecution and many are building new lives.'
— Peter Dutton, immigration minister

John Farmer, *Mercury*

Glen Le Lievre, *The Sun-Herald*

First Dog on the Moon, *The Guardian*

Fiona Katauskas, *Eureka Street*

'None of us have hearts of stone.'
— Malcolm Turnbull, PM

'Might I remind you when we closed down the live-animal export industry, it was around about the same time that we started seeing a lot of people arriving in boats in Australia ... I think it's absolutely the case that we created extreme bad will with Indonesia when we closed down the live-animal exports.'
— Barnaby Joyce, deputy PM

'No amount of moral lecturing from those who seem unable to comprehend the negative consequences of an open-borders policy will bring forth those solutions ... Yielding to emotional gestures in this area of public administration simply reduces the margin for discretionary action which is able to be employed by those people who are actually charged with dealing with the problem.'
— Mike Pezzullo, Immigration and Border Protection

Ron Tandberg, *The Age*

'We cannot be misty-eyed about this. We have to be very clear and determined in our national purpose.'
— Malcolm Turnbull, PM

Behrouz Boochani: What is my crime? I am a refugee who fled injustice, discrimination, and persecution. I didn't leave my family by choice. Why am I still in this illegal prison after three years?
Malcolm Turnbull: A person who has been found to be given refugee status in [Papua New Guinea] is able to then settle in PNG. I know, I'm sure, he would rather come to Australia, but that option is not available to him.

'When we wrote "continuity with change" the intention behind it was to write something as empty and as moronic sounding as possible … I'm praying for you guys over there.'
— Julia Louis-Dreyfus, *Veep*

Christopher Downes, *Mercury*

Andrew Dyson, *The Age*

John Spooner, *The Age*

Peter Broelman, *broelman.com.au*

Geoff Pryor, *The Saturday Paper*

'It is the biggest multilateral trade outcome for decades, and we will see big markets opening up for Australia whether it is in agriculture, or in services, or in manufacture — this is the foundation for our future prosperity ... our children's jobs depend on us having access to these big and growing markets, and this opens so many doors simultaneously, and, at the same time, we have preserved our vital national interests.'

— Malcolm Turnbull, PM

'I will stop any trade deal that kills jobs or holds down wages — including the Trans-Pacific Partnership. I oppose it now, I'll oppose it after the election, and I'll oppose it as president.'

— Hillary Clinton, US presidential candidate

Cathy Wilcox, *The Sun-Herald*

'We need to have in this country, and we will have now, an economic vision, a leadership that explains the great challenges and opportunities that we face, describes the way in which we can handle those challenges, seize those opportunities, and does so in a manner that the Australian people understand so that we are seeking to persuade rather than seeking to lecture.'
— Malcolm Turnbull, PM

'There is no easy answer to this; it does take years – it's Test Match, not Twenty20. I'm telling the Australian people that this will be a hard slog over a long period of time and you need to be disciplined and sober about it ... But we need to ensure we don't drag on that by putting taxes on people ... The best way to get ahead is to ensure expenditure is low, so taxes can remain low.'
— Scott Morrison, treasurer

Bruce Petty, *The Age*

Bruce Petty, *The Age*

Alan Moir, *The Sydney Morning Herald*

'We must increase and over time broaden the GST, we must lower all income tax ... Those people and companies are given more incentive to take risks and receive rewards. We should be wiser and more consistent on tax concessions to help pay for that; in particular, tax concessions on superannuation should be carefully pared back. In that framework, negative gearing should be skewed towards new housing so that there is an incentive to add to the housing stock rather than an incentive to speculate on existing property.'

— Joe Hockey valedictory speech

'We've all got a vested interest in there being an open debate, all things being on the table, nobody assuming that they've got the right answer. Of course, at the end of the day, the government has to make some decisions ... I'm not going to set out a timetable. I'm an activist, but I'm a thoughtful and considered activist.'

— Malcolm Turnbull, PM

Paul Zanetti, *www.zanetti.net.au*

Sean Leahy, *The Courier Mail*

Alan Moir, *The Sydney Morning Herald*

John Spooner, *The Age*

David Rowe, *Australian Financial Review*

'At this stage, I remain to be convinced or persuaded that a tax mix switch of that kind would actually give us the economic benefit you'd want in order to do such a big thing.'
— Malcolm Turnbull, PM

'The times are not right for that. We looked at it. We considered it. We did our homework. We assessed it. We put up with all the criticism and the flack and the noise and the turmoil because we wanted to make the right decision for the country. Had it been the right decision, then we would have done it.'
— Scott Morrison, treasurer

'Every tax deduction once created develops a constituency which will fight to defend it.'
— Malcolm Turnbull, MP, 2005

David Pope, *The Canberra Times*

Matt Golding, *The Sunday Age*

John Spooner, *The Age*

Jon Faine: [The kids are saying] for goodness sake, you baby boomers want everything and you're locking us out.
Malcolm Turnbull: Well, are your kids locked out of the housing market, Jon?
Jon Faine: Yes.
Malcolm Turnbull: Well, you should shell our for them, you should support them, a wealthy man like you.
Jon Faine: That's what *they* say.

'Is that really the prime minister's advice for young Australians struggling to buy their first home? Have rich parents?'
— Bill Shorten, opposition leader

David Rowe, *Australian Financial Review*

'I'm not going to try to sell the Australian public a unicorn, Alan, and say that there's really easy solutions here. You've just got to keep going at it, day in, day out, and that's what we're doing.'

— Scott Morrison, treasurer

'After five and half months in the job, treasurer Scott Morrison has finally made a clear and emphatic policy commitment: there will be no sale of unicorns on his watch. While some may find the treasurer's hardline on mythical creatures unusual, it is entirely consistent with this Liberal Government's fantasy approach to budgeting.'

— Andrew Leigh, shadow assistant treasurer

Andrew Dyson, *The Age*

Mark Knight, *Herald Sun*

Mark Knight, *Herald Sun*

Alan Moir, *The Sydney Morning Herald*

David Pope, *The Canberra Times*

'It was only last September when we started the approach of looking at superannuation, the GST, or other things like that. Those issues were not under consideration before September last year. It's not as if they were beavering away at them for two years before that. These issues only came into consideration in September last year.'

— Scott Morrison, treasurer

'In an ideal world, every level of government would raise itself from its own tax, taxes 100 per cent of the money it spends ... What we're talking about is the most fundamental reform to the Federation in generations.'

— Malcolm Turnbull, PM

'What's clear from today's pathetic performance by the treasurer is that it will be up to the Labor Party to continue to lead the debate because Australia has a treasurer who's simply not up it.'

— Chris Bowen, shadow treasurer

Pat Campbell, *The Canberra Times*

Cathy Wilcox, *The Sun-Herald*

Greg Smith, *The Sunday Times*

'He voted against it a year ago, Fran, but apparently in the eve of an election when there's a few reports about banks, Bill Shorten is up there in his ill-fitting suit, puffing his chest up, and saying we need to thump the table. This is just classic political distraction.'
— Scott Morrison, treasurer

'A building worker, a tradie, then the government is over them like a rash ... But the top end of town, the banks, the government is so quick out of the blocks to rule out a royal commission, it's breathtaking.'
— Bill Shorten, opposition leader

Peter Broelman, *broelman.com.au*

Andrew Dyson, *The Age*

John Spooner, *The Age*

'Wealth management as you deserve it.'
— Mossack Fonseca corporate slogan

'This is pretty much every document from this firm over a 40-year period ... about 2,000 times larger than the WikiLeaks state-department cables.'
— Gerard Ryle, International Consortium of Investigative Journalists

'Let me say to you that the company in which you Neville Wran and I were directors was an Australian-listed company, and had it made any profits, which it did not, regrettably, it certainly would have paid tax in Australia ... There is no suggestion of any impropriety whatsoever. There is nothing new there.'
— Malcolm Turnbull, PM

Alan Moir, *The Sydney Morning Herald*

'Remember this: The only way, the only way, we can ensure that we remain a high-wage, generous-social-welfare-net, first-world society is if we have outstanding economic leadership, if we have strong business confidence. That is what we, in the Liberal Party, are bound to deliver and it is what I am committed to deliver if the Party Room gives me their support as leader of the party.'
— Malcolm Turnbull, challenging Tony Abbott, 2015

'We say what we mean, we mean what we say, we do what we say we'd do in the way we say we'd do it.'
— Scott Morrison, treasurer

'Well, Malcolm's of course decided that the answer to every problem is more Malcolm. And what he wants to do is give the Australian people plenty of Malcolm over the next two months. Well, we'll see how that turns out.'
— Chris Bowen, shadow treasurer

Jon Kudelka, *www.kudelka.com.au*

Alan Moir, *The Sydney Morning Herald*

Bill Leak, *The Australian*

'If Turnbull sells out the Liberal Party to the Greens, he will return as a prime minister who owes nothing to the party's shattered conservatives, and will set about delivering same-sex marriage, a republic, a carbon trading scheme, and the rest of the left-liberal agenda, while setting himself up as Australia's first president. That's my hunch, anyway. But he will also set the stage for a third party to emerge from the right that will tap Trump-esque depths of anger. The forgotten people won't be ignored forever.'
— Miranda Devine, commentator

'It would be great to see someone leading the Liberal Party who hadn't been a member of the Labor Party [Brendan Nelson], hadn't contemplated joining the Labor Party [Turnbull, Hockey, Abbott], or wasn't a DLP supporter [Abbott].'
— Senator Cory Bernardi

'Who needs the Labor Party when you've got Andrew Bolt and the Delcons [delusional conservatives]?'
— anon Liberal

Paul Zanetti, *www.zanetti.net.au*

Pat Campbell, *The Canberra Times*

First Dog on the Moon,
The Guardian

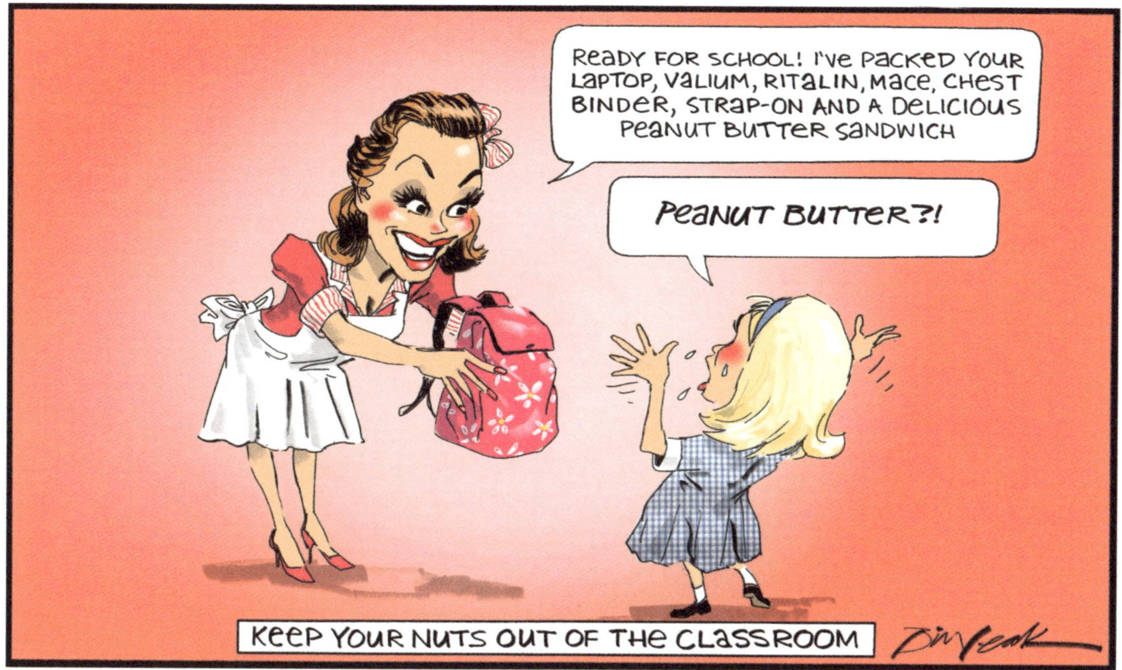

Bill Leak, *The Australian*

'Everyone who is attacking the Safe Schools work should calm down. It's designed to stop bullying … I think the PM should show leadership on a range of issues but he hasn't done it yet, so I'd be shocked if he does.'
— Terri Butler, Labor's child-safety spokeswoman

'North Korea gets schoolchildren to tip-off teachers and thereby the state that their parents have Bibles in their homes. Be very wary of those intolerant of different views when they start invading schools.'
— Senator Bob Day

'This material is putting children at risk of being sexualised at an early age. If a man exposed a child to these websites, sex clubs, sex shops, and online communities on the internet, we would call this a paedophile grooming a victim.'
— George Christensen, MP

Cathy Wilcox, *The Sun-Herald*

Alan Moir, *The Sydney Morning Herald*

Judy Horacek, *The Age*

'A plebiscite designed to deny me and many other Australians a marriage certificate will instead license hate speech to those who need little encouragement … Mr Turnbull, and many commentators on this subject, don't understand that for gay and lesbian Australians hate speech is not abstract. It's real. It's part of our everyday life.'

— Senator Penny Wong

'People of very strong religious views, they have also been subject to quite dreadful hate speech and bigotry as well. It is not confined to one side of this debate. I understand the concern Penny is raising — I know it from personal experience, having been exposed to that sort of hatred and bigotry for the views I've taken, from others who have a different view to me. But, that said, I have a bigger view of the Australian people … we can deal with this issue as a country once and for all and move on.'

— Scott Morrison, treasurer

Glen Le Lievre, *The Sun-Herald*

Fiona Katauskas, *Eureka Street*

David Pope, *The Canberra Times*

'This is a century of ideas, this is a time when Australia's growth, when our living standards, when our incomes will be determined by the human capital, the intellectual capital that all of us have. By unleashing our innovation, unleashing our imagination, being prepared to embrace change, we usher in the ideas boom. That is the next boom for Australia and, you know something, unlike a mining boom, it is a boom that can continue forever. It is limited only by our imagination, and I know that Australians believe in themselves; I know that we are a creative and imaginative nation, and — inspired, led, incentivised — we will have a very long ideas boom in the 21st century.'

— Malcolm Turnbull, PM

'Well, we're going to have an ideas boom after we get through the buffering ... When Malcolm Turnbull took over as communications minister, we were ranked 30 in terms of broadband speeds. Now we are ranked at 60. Most people would be demoted with a record like that — he got promoted to prime minister.'

— Ed Husic, MP

Andrew Weldon, *The Sunday Age*

Andrew Weldon, *The Sunday Age*

Ron Tandberg, *The Age*

'We've actually won. Me and Alan. We've house-trained Turnbull ... we knocked him into shape, Alan and I ... Behold our neo-Turnbull. Let the left weep.'
— Andrew Bolt, commentator

'It's a team business, and you have to keep the team together ... And when people say to me that I should just do whatever I like as though I'm some kind of dictator, they don't get it.'
— Malcolm Turnbull, PM

'A bit over six months ago the Liberal Party made you the PM on the promise that you weren't Tony Abbott ... but the real problem is that in two weeks you hope to continue in the same position on the argument that you're not Malcolm Turnbull either. Are you?'
— Glenn Wood, *Q&A*

Bill Leak, *The Australian*

Peter Broelman, *broelman.com.au*

Alan Moir, *The Sydney Morning Herald*

'Malcolm Turnbull had a plan to knock off Tony Abbott, but doesn't know what to do with [the leadership] afterwards ... What would be the point of a Turnbull government if it doesn't have a tax-reform agenda?'
— Chris Bowen, shadow treasurer

'It is fair to say that with the division and chaos that we have seen from Mr Turnbull's government, the prime minister is shrinking into his job.'
— Bill Shorten, opposition leader

'We were told that he would change the Liberal Party. But no, the Liberal Party has changed him from the moment he got that job.'
— Tony Burke, shadow environment minister

Jon Kudelka, *www.kudelka.com.au*

'Two-and-a-half years in government, more than five months as treasurer, and today we got 46 minutes of waffle, slogans, and platitudes from Scott Morrison. The only things left on the treasurer's much-vaunted table are incompetence, confusion, and indecision.'

— Chris Bowen, shadow treasurer

'Bill Shorten is very caring and very much in touch and Bill Shorten every single day is promoting our national economic plan for jobs and growth, which of course is exactly what Australia needs given the continued global economic headwinds.'

— Mathias Cormann, finance minister, accidentally backing the wrong leader

'The problem that the Labor Party has today is that Bill Shorten is an economic girlie man.'

— Mathias Cormann, finance minister

Mark Knight, *Herald Sun*

John Spooner, *The Age*

Jos Valdman, *The Advertiser*

'Given the critical importance of this industry to the nation, we now need and expect both sides of politics federally to make a similar commitment before the federal election.'

— Tom Koutsantonis, South Australian treasurer

'Christopher Pyne must level the playing field by stopping unfair imported-steel shipments or Whyalla will be reduced to little more than a coffee stop on the way from Adelaide to Port Lincoln.'

— Aaron Cartledge, CFMEU state secretary

'Governments at all levels ... spend a lot on infrastructure. What is wrong with requiring Australian content in the steel? ... I've represented steelworkers for the best part of 20 years. I understand that a nation that doesn't make its own steel loses a lot of its economic firepower.'

— Bill Shorten, opposition leader

Glen Le Lievre, *The Sun-Herald*

Ron Tandberg, *The Age*

Andrew Dyson, *The Age*

'This is a great day for our navy, a great day for Australia's 21st-century economy, a great day for the jobs of the future. Australian built, Australian jobs, Australian steel, here right where we stand.'
— Malcolm Turnbull, PM

'Our modelling and our plans clearly show us it is 1,100 jobs in the shipbuilding process, potentially 750 jobs in the supply-chain process, and that's without even taking into account the surface-ship announcement we made last week ... This is truly going to be a national endeavour.'
— Senator Marisa Payne

'I am pleased the shameful procrastination of the Labor years is now over. Australia's special relationship with Japan is more than strong enough to withstand this disappointment.'
— Tony Abbott, MP

John Farmer, *Mercury*

David Pope, *The Canberra Times*

Fiona Katauskas, *New Matilda*

Mark Knight, *Herald Sun*

'This is the right plan for Australia to overcome the challenges of economic transition and to clear a path for long-term growth and jobs in a stronger, new economy.'

— Scott Morrison, treasurer

'It could have been Chris Bowen making the case for tighter concessions on super, Tony Burke and Andrew Leigh pledging tougher action on multinationals, Michelle Rowland advocating a small-business tax cut, or Anthony Albanese outlining our new infrastructure approach. Never has an opposition had so many of its policies adopted by a government with so few of its own.'

— Bill Shorten, opposition leader

'There are currently $30 billion worth of "zombie" measures factored into the Liberals' Budget that will never pass Parliament.'

— Chris Bowen, shadow treasurer

John Spooner, *The Age*

Bill Leak, *The Australian*

'It was not a Budget full of giveaways and sweeteners. That is because this was not an election Budget — it was a Budget with the longer-term economic security of this country front of mind. We outlined our three clear aims: to deliver on our economic plan for jobs and growth; to ensure we have a sustainable tax system fit for the 21st century; to hold faithfully to a responsible, fair, and prudent approach to ensure the government lives within its means.'

— Malcolm Turnbull, PM

'From Tony's Tradies to Malcolm's Millionaires — this is a budget for big business over battlers.'

— Bill Shorten, opposition leader

'This budget was meant to be Malcolm Turnbull's justification for rolling Tony Abbott. After Tuesday night, Australians are left to wonder why he bothered.'

— Bill Shorten, opposition leader

David Rowe, *Australian Financial Review*

'The time for playing games is over ... I make no apology for interrupting senators' seven-week break to bring them back to deal with this legislation. This is an opportunity for the Senate to do its job of legislating rather than filibustering. The go-slows and obstruction by Labor and the Greens on this key legislation must end.'

— Malcolm Turnbull, PM

'What we've had today is the ghost of 1975 revisited upon us; the long, dead arm of Sir John Kerr crawling out of his grave to participate in a travesty of democracy in this country.'

— Senator Stephen Conroy

Mark Knight, *Herald Sun*

Mark Knight, *Herald Sun*

Christopher Downes, *Mercury*

'Today Mr Turnbull has decided to put his own future ahead of Australia's future. Today, Australians have seen a PM in full panic mode. There can be no better demonstration of the chaos at the heat of this dysfunctional and divided government than the fact that the treasurer of Australia thought that the Budget was going to be on a different day to his PM.'

— Bill Shorten, opposition leader

'The prime minister's threat of a double dissolution and an early election proves to all of us what this Budget is really about. It isn't about protecting the jobs of Australians, least of all the one million Australians it says will soon be out of work. It is about the job security of one man and one man only. A prime minister frightened of the consequences of his mismanagement now wants to cut and run before he is found out.'

— Malcolm Turnbull, opposition leader, 2009

First Dog on the Moon,
The Guardian

Fiona Katauskas, *New Matilda*

Glen Le Lievre, *The Sun-Herald*

Matt Golding, *The Sunday Age*

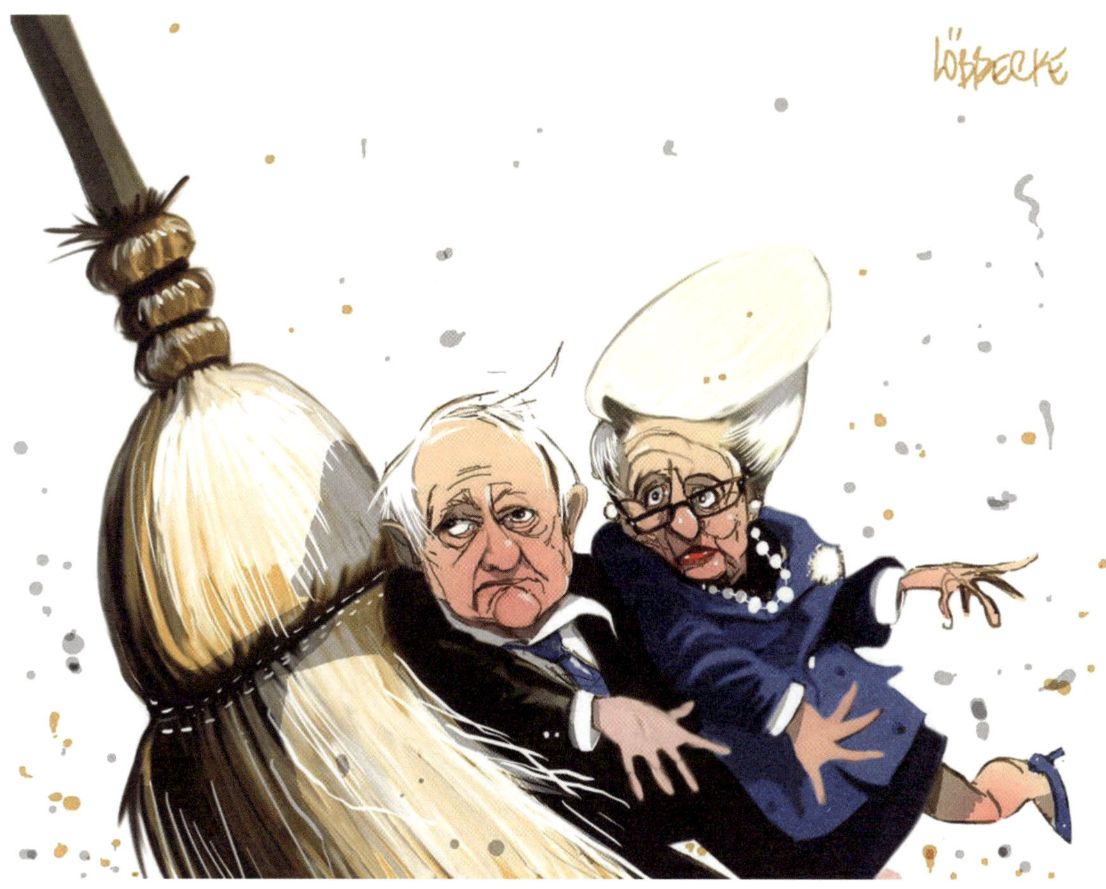

Eric Löbbecke, *The Australian*

'More disturbingly, a number of children have been thrown overboard — again, with the intention of putting us under duress. I regard these as some of the most disturbing practices that I have come across in the time that I have been involved in public life — clearly planned and premeditated.'
— Philip Ruddock, immigration minister, 2001

'As a distinguished member of the Australian Parliament for over four decades, the current chair of the parliamentary joint committee on human rights, and a longstanding member of Amnesty International, Mr Ruddock is well-qualified to advocate and represent Australia's human-rights views and record.'
— Julie Bishop, foreign minister

Sean Leahy, *The Courier Mail*

Fiona Katauskas, *Eureka Street*

Pat Campbell, *The Canberra Times*

Matt Golding, *The Sunday Age*

Jon Kudelka, *www.kudelka.com.au*

Sean Leahy, *The Courier Mail*

Mark Knight, *Herald Sun*

'We have already seen the Greening of Labor now, over many years. The Greening of Labor through the Rudd-Gillard-Rudd governments, and of course we have seen a very significant Greening of Labor under Bill Shorten – taken to a point where small business organisations say even the Greens would be better for small business than Labor.'

— Scott Morrison, treasurer

'Well, the Greens work with the Liberals as much as with anybody else. I mean, look at what's happening now. Where are the Greens putting their political energy? They're putting their political energy into defeating Labor MPs and candidates. How does that progress the progressive cause in Australia? I mean, how do they think it's a good thing for progressive Australia if they manage to defeat Anthony Albanese or Tanya Plibersek, for example? ... how does that help people who are interested in a more progressive Australia?'

— Chris Bowen, shadow treasurer

Mark Knight, *Herald Sun*

David Pope, *The Canberra Times*

Matt Golding, *The Sunday Age*

John Farmer, *Mercury*

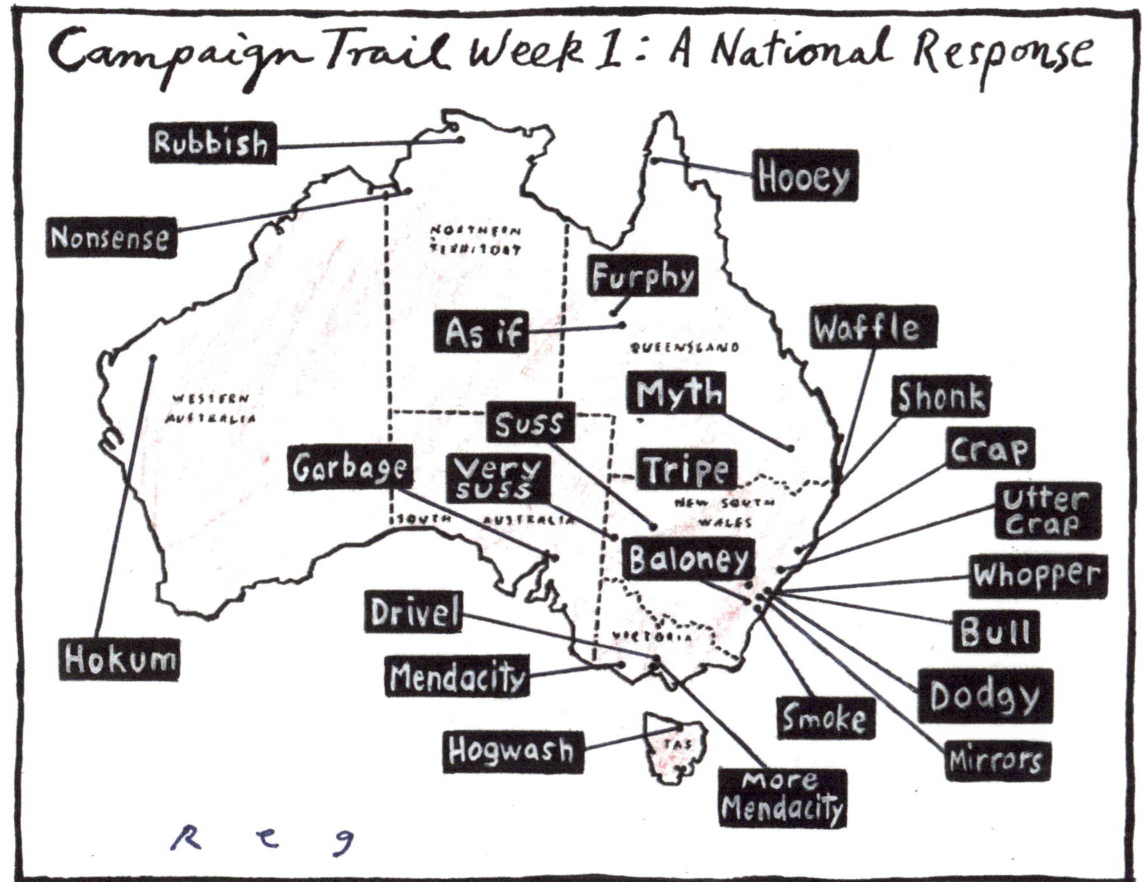

Reg Lynch, *The Sun-Herald*

'Political campaigning has deteriorated to such an extent that it treats politicians as consumer brands, similar to Coca-Cola or Pepsi. This trivialises politics and fuels cynicism.'
— Hugh Mackay, social researcher

'I think people are fed up with the cosy Coles–Woolies duopoly of the major parties; that they feel it is a case of Tweedledum and Tweedledee; that after seeing the so-called leaders' debate a couple of Sundays ago, it almost felt like the Seinfeld election — an election about not much at all.'
— Senator Nick Xenophon

Cathy Wilcox, *The Sun-Herald*

Dean Alston, *The West Australian*

Glen Le Lievre, *The Sun-Herald*

'I had a commitment for a $10 million allocation to the Wangaratta hospital that if elected I was going to announce the week after the election … That is $10 million that Wangaratta hasn't had because Cathy [McGowan] got elected.'

— Sophie Mirabella, Liberal candidate

'That's the sort of thing you see in a banana republic, not a functioning democracy.'

— Bill Shorten, opposition leader

'I think it's good to let taxpayers know that their money, a lot of which has gone into my professional development, has been well spent … David Morrison politicised the ADF long before I ever put my mug on a billboard.'

— Andrew Hastie, MP

David Rowe, *Australian Financial Review*

'What we've said is that we will announce the impact on the Budget of our measures over four years and ten. Right, the figures will be there for all to see. The size of the Budget deficits, the impact of our decisions over four years and ten. The question is, why won't Mr Morrison do the same? Where are his ten-year figures? Where are his ten-year figures and, yes, the government is claiming deficits over four years, both sides will have deficits over the next four years, they are claiming a figure which is a fantasy, based on zombie measures and retrospective taxes. We won't do that, that means we will have different deficit figures over those four years. We're saying that very clearly ...'

— Chris Bowen, shadow treasurer

John Spooner, *The Age*

'Labor will deliver bigger deficits over the four-year budget forward-estimates period, but they are asserting that somehow over the medium term they'll be able to pay for all of their unfunded spending promises. Labor has got a very bad track record here. In May 2012, Wayne Swan promised four years of surpluses and obviously by Christmas he had to fess up that there would be more deficits. What we've been saying for some time is they have a massive budget black hole, and today they're putting a lot of weasel words around fessing up that that is exactly what is happening.'

— Mathias Cormann, finance minister

John Farmer, *Mercury*

Glen Le Lievre, *The Sun-Herald*

Geoff Pryor, *The Saturday Paper*

'They won't be numerate or literate in their own language, let alone English. These people would be taking Australian jobs, there's no question about that. For many of them that would be unemployed, they would languish in unemployment queues and on Medicare and the rest of it, so there would be huge cost and there's no sense in sugar-coating that — that's the scenario.'

— Peter Dutton, immigration minister

'There are hundreds of thousands of refugees in Australia that have worked hard, who have educated themselves and their children, and they will be shaking their heads at their minister today in disgust, frankly.'

— Chris Bowen, shadow treasurer

David Pope, *The Canberra Times*

'Every home owner in Australia has a lot to fear from Bill Shorten.'
— Malcolm Turnbull, PM

'Let's envisage a [Parliament] with 150 independents. What we [would] have is total and utter chaos. That's the end of Australia. The Commonwealth will collapse.'
— Barnaby Joyce, deputy PM

'He was a great relief. How could you not be relieved? I was relieved. Their whole case to get rid of Tony Abbott was Abbott was trailing us. Malcolm's basic argument is "I speak well, I'm articulate. I've been an advocate for causes." But the problem is since he's got there, he's shrunk into the job. The common word I hear to describe the last eight months of Turnbull is *disappointment*. You can't say what you think your whole life, and then, when you get the chance to be in power and carry out the views people rate you for, say, "No I won't." ... They've just given in.'
— Bill Shorten, opposition leader

Andrew Weldon, *The Sunday Age*

Andrew Weldon, *The Sunday Age*

Cathy Wilcox, *The Sun-Herald*

Glen Le Lievre, *The Sun-Herald*

Reg Lynch, *The Sun-Herald*

'I've got a disability and a low education — that means I've spent my whole life working for minimum wage. You're gonna lift the tax-free threshold for rich people. If you lift my tax-free threshold, that changes my life. That means that I get to say to my little girls, "Daddy's not broke this weekend. We can go to the pictures." Rich people don't even notice their tax-free threshold lift. Why don't I get it? Why do they get it?'
— Duncan Storrar, *Q&A*

'Only the Liberal Party and the Labor Party can deliver. We're the only people that can form government. So independents, minor party, Greens, populist politicians, they can promise the world. Because they know they never have to deliver it.'
— Christopher Pyne, defence-industry minister

Paul Zanetti, *www.zanetti.net.au*

Dean Alston, *The West Australian*

Jon Kudelka, *www.kudelka.com.au*

'Bill Shorten even wants to go to war with someone like me, who just wants to get ahead through an investment property. Well, I tell you what happens when you get a war going on the economy: people like me lose their jobs.'

— Liberal TV commercial

'If it's known that you were going to do a street walk in Penrith, the last thing you want to do, "Mr Harbourside Mansion", is look like you don't know and you're not welcome in Western Sydney.'

— Peta Credlin, commentator

'Let me just say to you ... Lucy and I have been very lucky in our lives. We know that; we know there are many people who have worked harder that have not been so fortunate. We count our blessings and that's something that we recognise ... I can understand why Mr Shorten wants to make an issue of this. But I think that most Australians understand that our nation is built on opportunity and aspiration, and that all of us are entitled to aspire to achieve great things for our families.'

— Malcolm Turnbull, PM

Mark Knight, *Herald Sun*

'The aim of extremists, including those committing violence through a warped and nihilist interpretation of religion, is to divide us and to turn our citizens against each other — but we will not let them win ... We must stand together like we do tonight as one Australian family united against terrorism, racism, discrimination, and violence.'

— Malcolm Turnbull, PM

'We had the prime minister, Malcolm Turnbull, say Pauline Hanson has no place in Australian politics, and yet she represents the views or she reflects the concerns of many, many people — whether she does that well or badly is up for others to judge. Then we had circumstances where the prime minister was happy to hold and promote his inter-faith dinner and was more happy to be pictured with Waleed Aly than with the conservative base of the Liberal Party.'

— Senator Cory Bernardi

Fiona Katauskas, *New Matilda*

David Pope, *The Canberra Times*

'It's 24 hours away from the election — we still have 24 hours to ensure we can save Medicare.'
— Bill Shorten, opposition leader

'I have seen amazing things, but the discussion about the privatisation of Medicare just takes the cake. Why don't we say that the Labor Party will cut the Sydney Harbour Bridge in two and move it to Tamworth and we will stop it. It is a load of garbage. It is just made up.'
— Barnaby Joyce, deputy PM

"We had GetUp spending and bragging about the fact they spent $500,000 just in the seat of Bass, with ten full-time people besmirching the character of a great Australian servant.'
— Senator Eric Abetz

'There was some fertile ground in which that grotesque lie could be sown. There is no doubt about that.'
— Malcolm Turnbull, PM

Christopher Downes, *Mercury*

Dean Alston, *The West Australian*

Geoff Pryor, *The Saturday Paper*

'This is a critical choice. This is going to be a close election … all federal elections are close, as we know. But this is a time of great moment for Australia. There has never been a clearer choice in a generation. This is the most anti-business Labor Party platform that we have seen. We've seen Labor has declared a war on business, and the first casualties are jobs. We have a clear policy for jobs and growth, a stable government, and that's the choice we urge Australians to make on July 2 and right up to that date if they are voting early.'

— Malcolm Turnbull, PM

'That is an unworthy scare campaign from Mr Turnbull, who vowed to be different to Tony Abbott. Now Malcolm Turnbull's channelling his inner Tony Abbott.'

— Bill Shorten, opposition leader

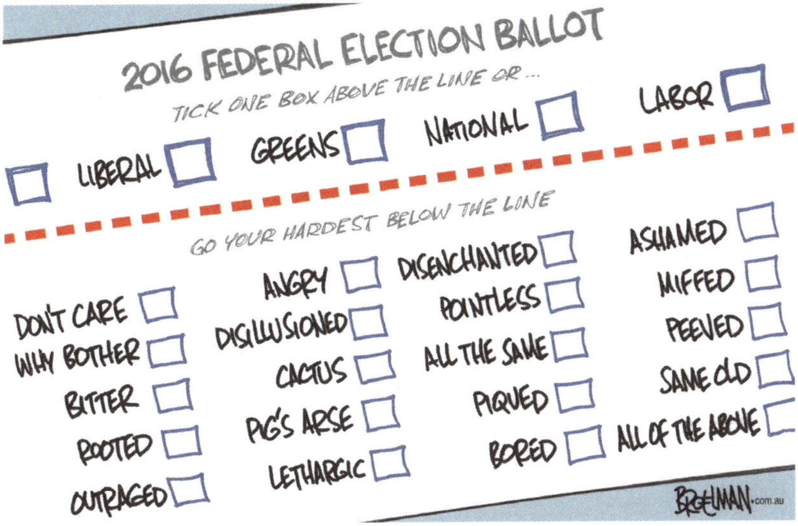

2016 FEDERAL ELECTION BALLOT
TICK ONE BOX ABOVE THE LINE OR ...
LIBERAL
GREENS
NATIONAL
LABOR
GO YOUR HARDEST BELOW THE LINE
DON'T CARE
WHY BOTHER
BITTER
ROOTED
OUTRAGED
ANGRY
DISILLUSIONED
CACTUS
PIG'S ARSE
LETHARGIC
DISENCHANTED
POINTLESS
ALL THE SAME
PIQUED
BORED
ASHAMED
MIFFED
PEEVED
SAME OLD
ALL OF THE ABOVE
BROELMAN.com.au

Peter Broelman, *broelman.com.au*

Paul Zanetti, *www.zanetti.net.au*

Pat Campbell, *The Canberra Times*

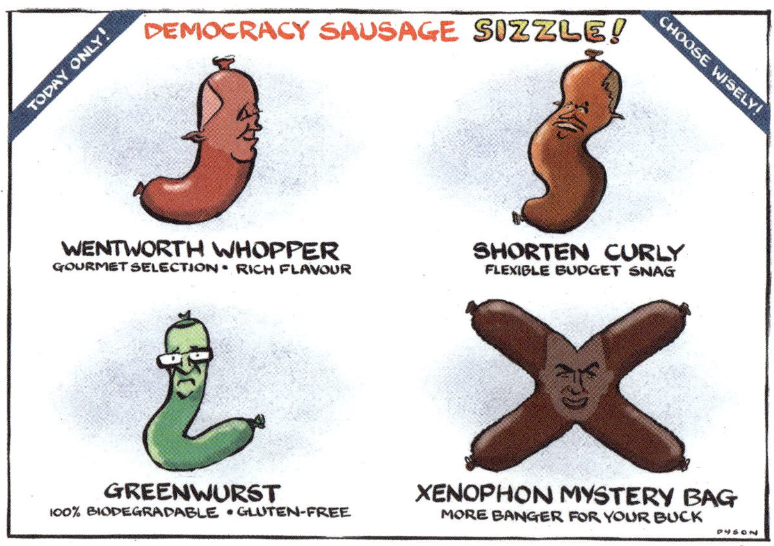

Andrew Dyson, *The Age*

Andrew Dyson, *The Age*

'Tony Abbott must return as leader of the shattered Liberals after Saturday's election disaster. Prime Minister Malcolm Turnbull out, Abbott in – even if journalists still sneer.

'True, Abbott ideally needs months more to repair the image that a smart-arse media tore to shreds, feeding off his sometimes dumb mistakes. But who else but Abbott could hope to fix what Turnbull has just smashed?

'This election result has been a near-total catastrophe for the Liberals, who have been left without a mandate, platform, unity, honour, or real power after letting Turnbull hijack their party last year. Turnbull, a man of the ABC Left, then ditched the Liberals' base, Liberal principles, and even the Liberals' party colours to campaign on virtually nothing but a fantasy tax cut for business. Now look at the smoking ruin.'

– Andrew Bolt, commentator

Bill Leak, *The Australian*

Sean Leahy, *The Courier Mail*

Matt Golding, *The Sunday Age*

'Malcolm might be watching the Channel 7 broadcast and if you are Malcolm ... come and face the people.'
— Alan Jones, commentator

'It's the first time I've seen a bloke who's probably won the election say "We was robbed". I thought that quite frankly was pretty pathetic. It was an angry, bitter speech from a bloke who only two days ago promised a different sort of politics because Australians, he said, were quite sick of the personal stuff, the rancorous stuff — that's what we got tonight.'
— Lawrie Oakes, journalist

'Tonight, my friends, I can report that based on the advice I have from the party officials, we can have every confidence we will form a Coalition majority government in the next Parliament.'
— Malcolm Turnbull, PM

David Rowe, *Australian Financial Review*

'If you think you can govern Australia with 76 members of parliament, I wish you well! No one can go to the bathroom! Don't have your grandmother die, because you won't be able to go to the funeral!'
— Bob Katter, MP

'The truth is Labor lost the election. The Liberal Party won it. It's our sixth victory out of the last eight. We are the Hawthorn of Australian politics.'
— Christopher Pyne, defence-industry minister

'I have not heard a single sensible reason for keeping the Coalition deal a secret. This is not internal party business. It is national business, and the nation deserves to know what deals are being done.'
— Bill Shorten, opposition leader

Eric Löbbecke, *The Australian*

Greg Smith, *The Sunday Times*

Warren Brown, *The Daily Telegraph*

'Malcolm Turnbull, you are the man that broke the Liberal Party's heart ... Everyone has had crack at me and the advice I gave the prime minister, Tony Abbott, but at least he won an election.'
— Peta Credlin, commentator

'It's nine months ago that Malcolm Turnbull assassinated Tony Abbott promising only one thing — that he would do better than Tony Abbott at the polls.'
— Andrew Bolt, commentator

'A lot of us held our noses, sold it during the election campaign.'
— Eric Abetz, MP

'It's not the end of the world, and people shouldn't start slitting their throats, certainly not Liberals.'
— John Howard

Alan Moir, *The Sydney Morning Herald*

David Rowe, *Australian Financial Review*

David Pope, *The Canberra Times*

'The Labor Party, the Labor Party ran some of the most systematic, well-funded lies ever peddled in Australia.'

— Malcolm Turnbull, PM

'I think that the thing that made the difference … was the fact that the Labor Party threw the kitchen sink at one of the most mendacious and disgraceful campaigns that we've ever seen … The proposition that the government planned to sell or privatise Medicare was … a nonsense.'

— Senator George Brandis

'Clearly, a wafer thin majority requires the prime minister and the leadership not only to reach out to the cross benchers but also all elements within the Liberal National Party coalition because I'm sure they must realise it will only take one person or two in the House of Representatives to cross the floor to defeat government legislation.'

— Eric Abetz, MP

Sean Leahy, *The Courier Mail*

Alan Moir, *The Sydney Morning Herald*

Geoff Pryor, *The Saturday Paper*

'His theory was to win and win comfortably so the conservatives would all have to kneel at the altar of Malcolm Turnbull; well, I think someone else will be kneeling at the conservative altar now.'
— Coalition MP, anon.

'As of writing, over 1.7 million votes were cast for right-of-centre or conservative parties rather than the Liberal Party. From my perspective, that was the Liberal base expressing their unhappiness with past events. Irrespective of the final election result, the clear mission now is to bring people together for the good of the country. That is going to take the formalisation of a broad conservative movement to help change politics and to give common sense a united voice.'
— Cory Bernardi, MP

David Rowe, *Australian Financial Review*

Alan Jones: There were a lot of bed-wetters in the Liberal Party, and you seem to be the captain of the bed-wetters. The reality is that in 2010 Abbott won seven seats from Labor and in 2013 he won 18. In two elections, he won 25 seats. I would have thought that that, on the basis of winning elections, was pretty good form. So now your Queanbeyan mob, Peter Hendy and Co, whom you organised and coordinated and led while Tony Abbott was in Adelaide, have now got to confront this. The Liberal Party out there will be very, very distressed about what's happened.

Senator James McGrath: Alan, I actually don't care what you think, because you're not a friend of conservatives, you're not a friend of the Liberal National Party. You're the king of the bed-wetters, actually. You are actually a grub.

Ron Tandberg, *The Age*

Ron Tandberg, *The Age*

Anton Emdin, *The Spectator Australia*

Tony Abbott: All sorts of things might happen in the future, but right now you've got to be content with serving your electorate.
Andrew Bolt: I didn't hear a 'no' in there, Tony.

Peter Nicholson, *nicholsoncartoons.com.au*

'Napoleon, Hitler, various people tried this out, and it ends tragically. The EU is an attempt to do this by different methods.'

— Boris Johnson, UK MP

Warren Brown, *The Daily Telegraph*

Pat Campbell, *The Canberra Times*

Dean Alston, *The West Australian*

'Hillary wants to abolish, essentially abolish the Second Amendment ... By the way, and if she gets to pick if she gets to pick her judges, nothing you can do, folks. Although the Second Amendment people, maybe there is. I don't know. But I'll tell you what, that will be a horrible day.'

— Donald Trump, presidential candidate

'Nobody who is seeking a leadership position, especially the presidency, the leadership of the country, should do anything to countenance violence, and that's what he was saying ... a window into the soul of a person who is just temperamentally not suited to the task.'

— Senator Tim Kaine, vice-presidential candidate

'This isn't play. Unstable people with powerful guns and an unhinged hatred for Hillary are listening to you.'

— Senator Chris Murphy

Peter Nicholson, *The Australian*

Andrew Dyson, *The Age*

Geoff Pryor, *The Saturday Paper*

Bruce Petty, *The Age*

David Rowe, *Australian Financial Review*

'Now, finally friends, I want you to try to picture this — it's a nice thing to picture. Exactly one year from tomorrow, former president Barack Obama. He packs up the teleprompters and the selfie-sticks, and the Greek columns, and all that hopey, changey stuff, and he heads on back to Chicago, where I'm sure he can find some community there to organise again. There, he can finally look up, and there, over his head, he'll be able to see that shining, towering Trump tower.'

— Sarah Palin

'In fact, in many respects, you know they honour President Obama, ISIS is honouring President Obama. He is the founder of ISIS. He is the founder of ISIS. He's the founder. He founded ISIS. And I would say the co-founder would be crooked Hillary Clinton. Co-founder. Crooked Hillary Clinton.'

— Donald Trump, presidential candidate

David Rowe, *Australian Financial Review*

'[Donald Trump ...] Go look at the graves of brave patriots who died defending the United States of America. You will see all faiths, genders, and ethnicities. You have sacrificed nothing and no one.'
— Khizr Khan, Democratic convention

'I've made a lot of sacrifices. I work very, very hard. I've created thousands and thousands of jobs, tens of thousands of jobs, built great structures. I've had tremendous success. I think I've done a lot.'
— Donald Trump, presidential candidate

'Putin has much better leadership qualities than Obama ... I said he's a better leader than Obama, because Obama's not a leader, so he's certainly doing a better job than Obama is, and that's all.'
— Donald Trump, presidential candidate

David Rowe, *Australian Financial Review*

Cathy Wilcox, *The Sun-Herald*

Matt Golding, *The Sunday Age*

Mark Knight, *Herald Sun*

David Rowe, *Australian Financial Review*

'She knows what it's like to be the subject of the stereotype that a powerful woman cannot be likable, that if she is commanding then she must be incapable of empathy.'

— Julia Gillard

'That is the story of this country. The story that has brought me to this stage tonight. The story of generations of people who felt the lash of bondage, the shame of servitude, the sting of segregation, but who kept on striving and hoping and doing what needed to be done — so that today I wake up every morning in a house that was built by slaves.'

— Michelle Obama

Reg Lynch, *The Sun-Herald*

'I defend that decision … I don't retreat from it. I don't believe that, on the basis of the information that was available to me, it was the wrong decision. I really don't.'
— John Howard

'Howard has visited on Australia the whole spectre of terrorism, through his craven and ill-judged support of the United States and its invasion.'
— Paul Keating

'There will not be a day when I do not relive and rethink what happened … I believe we made the right decision and the world is better and safer.'
— Tony Blair

Cathy Wilcox, *The Sun-Herald*

Pat Campbell, *The Canberra Times*

Sean Leahy, *The Courier Mail*

Greg Smith, *The Sunday Times*

Cathy Wilcox, *The Sun-Herald*

Cathy Wilcox, *The Sun-Herald*

David Rowe, *Australian Financial Review*

'China will take all necessary measures to protect its territorial sovereignty and maritime rights and interests.'

— *People's Daily*

'Australia stands with the international community in calling for both sides to treat the arbitral ruling as final and binding.'

— Julie Bishop, foreign minister

'The treasurer's decision yesterday is a huge concession — the first major policy sacrifice — to the witches' sabbath of xenophobia and economic nationalism stirred up in the recent federal election.'

— Bob Carr, on Ausgrid decision

Andrew Dyson, *The Age*

Alan Moir, *The Sydney Morning Herald*

Reg Lynch, *The Sun-Herald*

'Well, I think it can be fairly described as that, and I've got no doubt obviously our first Aboriginal Australians describe it as an invasion. But, you know, you are talking about an historical argument about a word. The facts are very well known. This country was Aboriginal land. It was occupied by Aboriginal people for tens of thousands of years — 40,000 years.'

— Malcolm Turnbull, PM

'I certainly wouldn't use the word "invasion". The terminology I use is "settlement". If that's too benign, fair enough, say Australia was occupied if you like.'

— Tony Abbott, MP

David Rowe, *Australian Financial Review*

'It shouldn't be strange or unusual for people of Pat's renown, experience, and wisdom to be given the chance to serve in our parliament, but at the moment it is.'
— Bill Shorten, opposition leader

'I want to ensure that people in the remote areas and in the northern areas of Australia are also able to enjoy the services and the quality of those services that we can enjoy in cities and other places ... In particular, the constitutional recognition of the first peoples of this nation, and getting to a stage where our nation can put behind us those causes of division and discord that have so divided so many of us from enjoying the fullness and the fruits and the benefits that this nation's got to offer.'
— Senator Pat Dodson

Ron Tandberg, *The Age*

Cathy Wilcox, *The Sun-Herald*

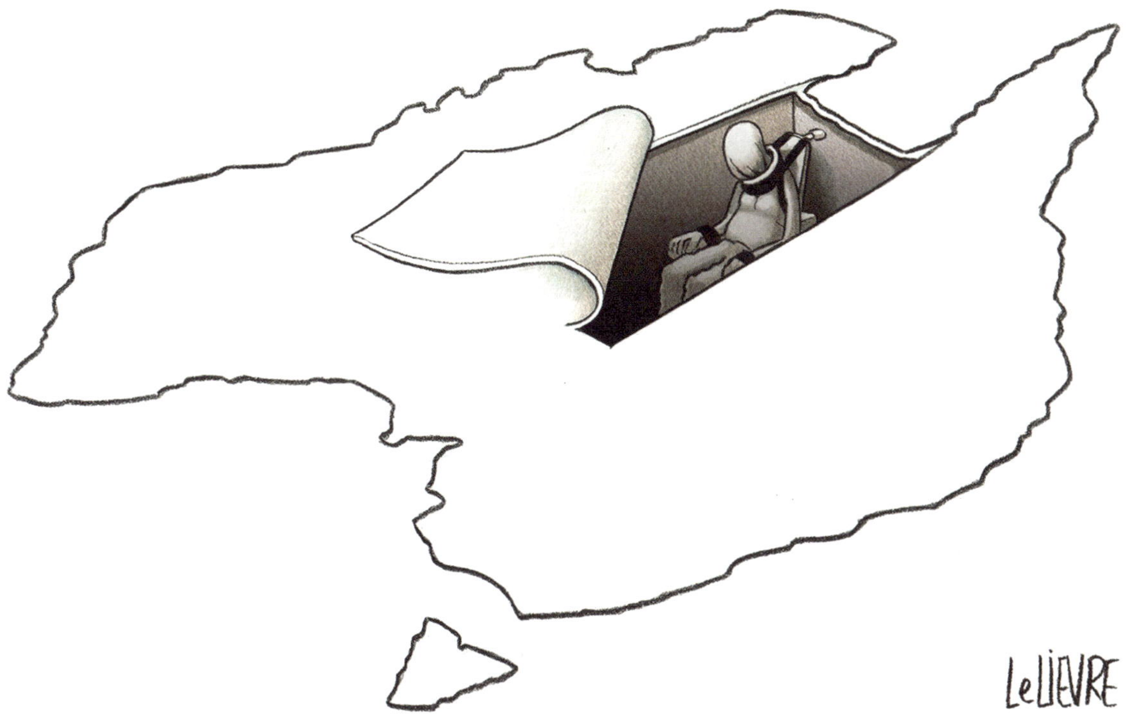

Glen Le Lievre, *The Sun-Herald*

'It's a sad story, and it wasn't of much interest to me.'
— Cardinal George Pell

'I had never seen the vision. It hadn't come to my attention, hadn't piqued my interest sufficiently.'
— Nigel Scullion, Indigenous affairs minister

'If I was the prisons minister, I would build a big concrete hole and put all the bad criminals in there ... I might break every United Nations' convention on the rights of the prisoner, but, "Get in the hole."'
— Adam Giles, MP, 2010

'We've seen an outrageous report just a couple of weeks ago now about Don Dale ... To see an episode such as that try and stir up racial divide in the Northern Territory, I think is appalling, I think it's racist, and I'm absolutely disgusted in what they've done.'
— Adam Giles, NT chief minister

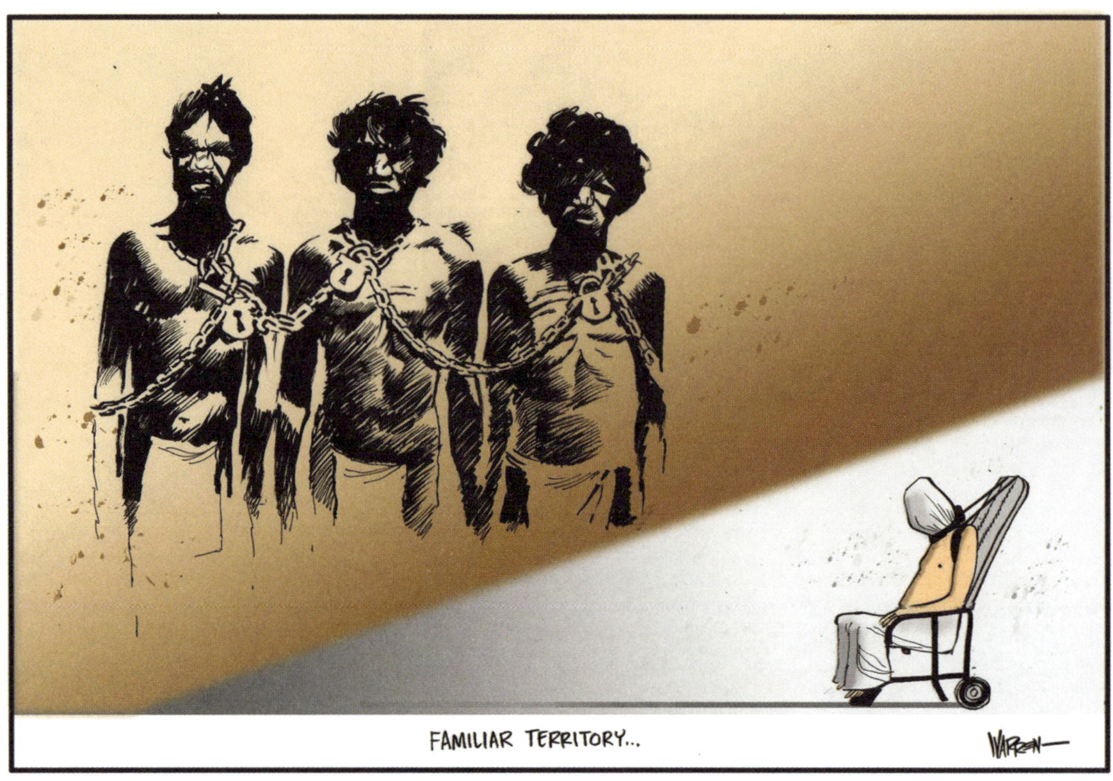

Warren Brown, *The Daily Telegraph*

'There's always a problem with depicting Indigenous people in cartoons because grotesque caricature has such a poisonous history in Australia. But then what happened to those kids in jail — and what happened before they got there in some cases — is grotesque.'

— Warren Brown, cartoonist

'I share everybody's distress about it ... But I have to say: we can't allow as Australians our outrage to be selective. We should be outraged about those things that are driving the large numbers of those tragic juveniles, who were once little babies, who were once little toddlers, and who have ended up with a bag over their head, being abused in an institution ...

'I think Australians have become so inured to this problem that it is literally something that, unless you see very graphic images on television, we are largely unmoved.'

— Noel Pearson, Cape York Indigenous leader

First Dog on the Moon,
The Guardian

Fiona Katauskas, *New Matilda*

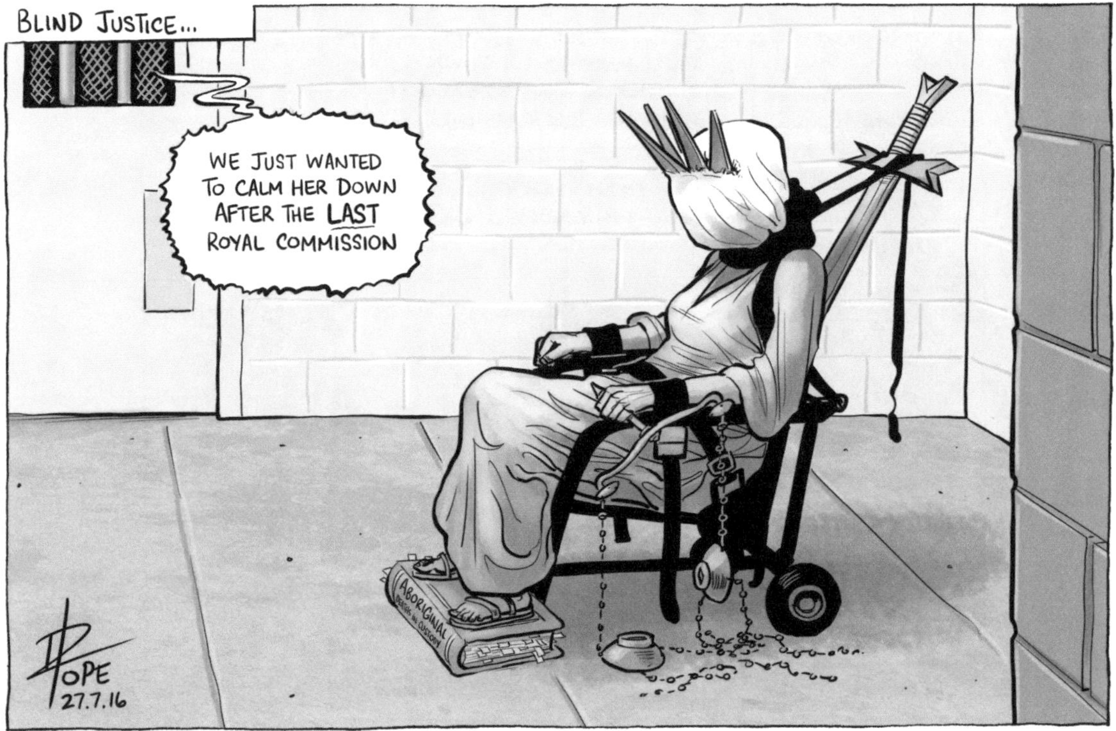

David Pope, *The Canberra Times*

'It has become apparent that, rightly or wrongly, in this role I would not have the full confidence of sections of the Indigenous community, which has a vital interest in this inquiry.'
— Brian Martin, resigning royal commissioner

'The federal government has to intervene and sack the NT government.'
— Mick Gooda, ATSI social justice commissioner

'You will not find an Indigenous leader in this country who hasn't had some sharp and strong things to say about the way in which the system treats Indigenous youth.'
— Senator George Brandis

'The appropriateness of the appointments is the subject of debate but suffice it to say that ... I am most surprised that ancestry seems a more important qualification than judicial experience.'
— Senator Cory Bernardi

Bill Leak, *The Australian*

'Blackfellas have got to take charge and take responsibility for their own children.'
— Noel Pearson, Cape York Indigenous leader

'The cartoon I drew for yesterday's paper was inspired by Indigenous men and people who, without regard for their personal safety, feel compelled to tell the truth.'
— Bill Leak, cartoonist

'Bill claims to be the great revealer of the truth. Only he dares to say what the rest of us deny, that Aboriginal people are responsible for their own social disadvantage ... The trouble with that is it ignores some fundamental "truths" about how they came to be disadvantaged ... I still defend his right to say it.'
— Cathy Wilcox, cartoonist

'Not only do I know my son's name, but I named a superhero after him. #IndigenousDads #Cleverman'
— Ryan Griffen, Twitter

David Pope, *The Canberra Times*

'Bill Leak ... was subjected to a vile campaign of intimidation. Government-funded organisations trashed his reputation and reported him for punishment. Those responsible are misusing state power to bully people into silence. They are cowards, scared of debate. And for all their sanctimonious tears for Aborigines, they are hypocrites, wilfully blind to the suffering of a truly stolen generation of Aboriginal children.'

— Andrew Bolt, commentator

'It was clearly racist and it reminded me of the sorts of cartoons we saw in the 1920s and 1930s in national newspapers.'

— Andrew Meehan, Australians for Native Title and Reconciliation (ANTaR)

'If you want to take offence, that's your choice. You have the choice of choosing another feeling. Offence is always taken, not given. So if you don't want to be offended, you, it's up to you; don't be offended ... We're not responsible for the feelings of other people, none of us are.'

— Senator David Leyonhjelm

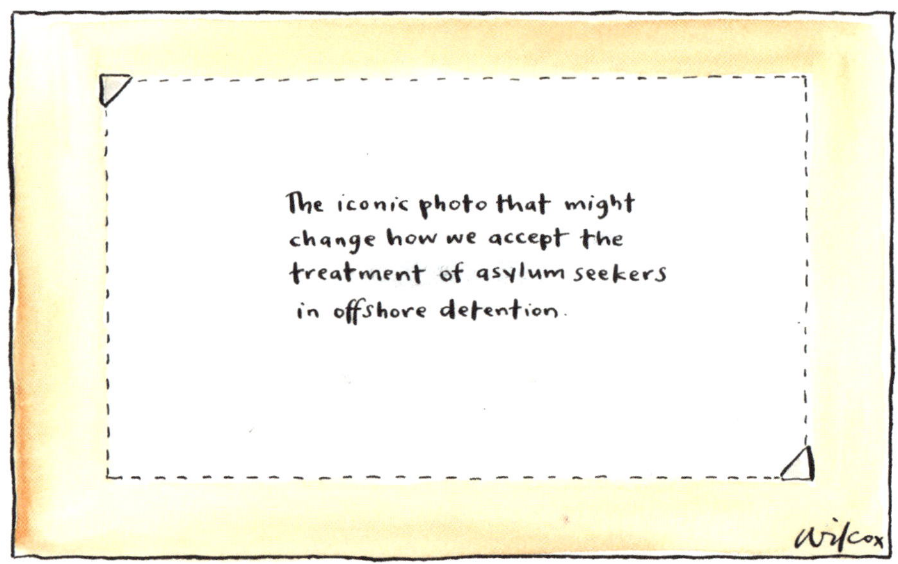

Cathy Wilcox, *The Sun-Herald*

Sean Leahy, *The Courier Mail*

Ron Tandberg, *The Age*

'There is a real hypocrisy in the fact we have two royal commissions currently afoot – one into institutional child sexual abuse and another into youth detention centres – and yet at the very same time we're warehousing children on Nauru in conditions that allow this kind of abuse to thrive.'
– Hugh de Kretser, Human Rights Law Centre

'I won't tolerate any sexual abuse whatsoever. But I have been made aware of some incidents that have been reported, false allegations of sexual assault, because in the end people have paid money to people smugglers and they want to come to our country.'
– Peter Dutton, immigration minister

'Our democratic system depends on transparency and access by our journalists and also by other community groups who can speak up and take photographs. That is what really moves the public, when they actually see, preferably on video, how these children are being treated.'
– Gillian Triggs, Australian Human Rights Commission

First Dog on the Moon,
The Guardian

Jon Kudelka, *www.kudelka.com.au*

'I believe that as the other candidates are former leaders, former prime ministers, former foreign ministers of their country, then he is qualified to be a candidate.'
— Julie Bishop, foreign minister

'When the Australian government nominates a person for a job, particularly an international job like this, the threshold question is, "Do we believe the person, the nominee, the would-be nominee is well suited for that position?" My judgement is that Mr Rudd is not.'
— Malcolm Turnbull, PM

'Whatever I'd say about Malcolm Turnbull, he's not petty and mean-spirited like that, so he's bowed to pressure from the blue blues.'
— Bob Katter, MP

'It's no small thing when the prime minister of Australia stands up and says that one of his prime ministerial predecessors is unsuitable to be considered as a candidate for UN secretary-general.'
— Kevin Rudd

Jon Kudelka, *www.kudelka.com.au*

'We filled in the @ABSCensus tonight online - v easy to do. And so important for planning better Govt services & investment for the future.'

— Malcolm Turnbull, PM, Twitter

'It was an attack, and we believe from overseas ... it was quite clear it was malicious.'

— David Kalisch, chief statistician

'There was some anomalous traffic on the night that appeared to be anomalous. Actually it was quite innocent, it turned out, but that caused the ABS to take the site down.'

— Malcolm Turnbull, PM

'I will be clear from the outset: This was not an attack. Nor was it a hack but rather, it was an attempt to frustrate the collection of Bureau of Statistics Census data.'

— Michael McCormack, small business minister

David Pope, *The Canberra Times*

Andrew Dyson, *The Age*

Fiona Katauskas, *Eureka Street*

Fiona Katauskas, *Eureka Street*

Jon Kudelka, *www.kudelka.com.au*

'You're standing here having a go at me because I stand up for my culture, my way of life, and my country.'
— Senator Pauline Hanson

'David Leyonhjelm is a boorish, supercilious know-all with the empathy of a besser block. And that new Hansonite conspiracy theorist from Queensland? He's an absurdist fringe-dweller and fellow hate-speech apologist. It's a case of wacky and wackier … Presumably, both of these giants of the legislature will choose to be "very happy" about being named as rank apologists for the resentment industry promoted by angry-white-male shock jocks and TV Tea Party types.'
— Mark Kenny, journalist

'Assuming the adjudicators at the Human Rights Commission are guided by the law and not racists, I anticipate the complaint should succeed. Of course, if I succeed in having section 18C repealed, Mr Kenny will be free to insult me as much as he likes.'
— Senator David Leyonhjelm

David Pope, *The Canberra Times*

'No matter how narrow the outcome, whether it be one-hundredth of a second, whether it be one goal, one percentage point, if you cross that line first you get to stand on the top podium, you get the gold medal ... A win is a win.'

— Julie Bishop, foreign minister

'Someone came up with an idea to put squat toilets into the new Australian Tax Office in Melbourne ... if they can't work out how to use a Westernised toilet, how are they expected to work out our tax system and give advice to ordinary Australians? ... It's not just a matter of dollars ... It starts with toilets and ends with costing us our Australian way of life.'

— Senator Pauline Hanson

'Would you have allowed five-year-old Sam Dastyari into this country?'

— Senator Sam Dastyari

Matt Golding, *The Sunday Age*

Christopher Downes, *Mercury*

Bruce Petty, *The Age*

'I've always had a feeling you've got to tie everything together. Everything fits somehow ... I'm trying to put the history in, and I have a feeling that if you explain it, it will look good. There will be an aesthetic. My dad was good at machinery, and on the orchard we built a lot of machinery. If you do something here, it'll pull that lever, tip this over, and that'll turn that. It's a weird metaphor because it isn't really what humans do, but you can make it a metaphor for human behaviour.'

'There are so many tantalising things to do. I'll be battling away with some dopey idea until they drag me away to the clinic.'

— Bruce Petty, retired from *The Age,* 2016